Historical Notices Of Edward And William Christian: Two Characters In Peveril Of The Peak

James Marsden

In the interest of creating a more extensive selection of rare historical book reprints, we have chosen to reproduce this title even though it may possibly have occasional imperfections such as missing and blurred pages, missing text, poor pictures, markings, dark backgrounds and other reproduction issues beyond our control. Because this work is culturally important, we have made it available as a part of our commitment to protecting, preserving and promoting the world's literature. Thank you for your understanding.

HISTORICAL NOTICES

OF

Edward and William Christian;

TWO CHARACTERS

IN

PEVERIL OF THE PEAK.

B. Bensley, Bolt Court, Fleet Street.

HISTORICAL NOTICES.

The venerable Dr. Dryasdust, in a preparatory dialogue, apprizes the Eidolon, or apparition of the author, that he stood "much accused for adulterating the pure sources of historical knowledge;" and is answered by that emanation of genius, "that he has done some service to the public if he can present to them a lively fictitious picture, for which the original anecdote or circumstance which he made free to press into his service, only furnished a slight sketch;" "that by introducing to the busy and the youthful

'Truths severe in fairy fiction dressed,'

and by creating an interest in fictitious adventures ascribed to a historical period and characters, the reader begins next to be anxious *to learn what the facts really were*, and how far the novelist has justly represented them."

The adventures ascribed to "historical characters" would however fail in their moral aim, if fiction were placed at variance with truth; if Hampden, or Sydney, for example, were painted as swindlers; or Lady Jane Grey, or Rachel Russel, as abandoned women!

"Odzooks! must one swear to the truth of a song?" although an excellent joke, were a bad palliation in such a case. Fancy may be fairly indulged in the illustration, but not in the perversion of fact; and if the fictitious picture should have no general resemblance to the original, the flourish of

"Truths severe in fairy fiction dressed"

were but an aggravation of the wrong.

The family of CHRISTIAN is indebted to this splendid luminary of the North for abundant notoriety.

The William Christian, represented on one part as an ungrateful traitor, on the other as the victim of a judicial murder, and his brother (or relative) Edward, one of the suit of a Duke[1] of Buckingham, were so far real historical persons.

---

[1] Not the Duke described in Peveril, but the companion of Charles I. in his Spanish romance.

Whether the talents and skill of Edward in imposing on Fenella a feigned silence of several years, be among the legitimate or supernatural wonders of this fertile genius, his fair readers do not seem to be agreed. Whether the residue of the canvas, filled up with a masterly picture of the most consummate hypocrite and satanic villain ever presented to the imagination, be consistent with the historical character of this individual, is among the subjects of research to which the novelist has given a direct invitation in his prefatory chapter.

English history furnishes few materials to aid the investigation of transactions chiefly confined to the Isle of Man. Circumstances led me, many years ago, to visit this ancient Lilliput; whether as one of those " smart fellows worth talking to," " in consequence of a tumble from my barouche," " as a ruined miner," or as " a disappointed speculator," is of no material import. It may be that temporary embarrassment drove me into seclusion, without any of the irresistible inducements alluded to; and want of employment, added to the acquaintance and aid of a zealous local antiquary, gradually led to an examination of all accessible authorities on this very subject among others. So it happened, that I had not landed many hours before I found the mournful ditty of "William Dhône," (*brown* or *fair-haired William*, this very identical William Christian,) twanged through the demi-nasal, demi-guttural trumpet of the carman, and warbled by the landlady's pretty daughter; in short, making as great a figure in its little sphere as did once the more important ballad of Chevy Chace in its wider range: the burden of the song purporting that William Dhône was the mirror of virtue and patriotism, and that envy, hatred, and malice, and all uncharitableness, operate the destruction of the wisest and the best.

Themes of popular feeling naturally attract the earliest notice of a stranger; and I found the story of this individual, though abundantly garbled and discoloured on the insular records, full of circumstances to excite the deepest interest, but which, to be rendered intelligible, must be approached by a circuitous route, in which neither elfin, page, nor maiden fair, can be the companion of our walk.

The loyal and celebrated James, 7th Earl of Derby, was induced, by the circumstances of the times, to fix his chief residence in the Isle of

Man from 1643 to 1651.[2] During this period he composed, in the form of a letter[3] to his son Charles (Lord Strange,) an historical account of that island, with a statement of his own proceedings there; interspersed with much political advice for the guidance of his successor; full of acute observation, and evincing an intimate acquaintance with the works of Machiavelli, which it appears, by a quotation,[4] that he had studied in a Latin edition. The work, although formally divided into chapters and numbered paragraphs, is professedly desultory,[5] and furnishes few means

---

[2] His countess resided at Latham House (her heroic defence of which is well known) until 1644 or 5, when she also retired to the Isle of Man. A contemporary publication, the *Mercurius Aulicus*, by John Birkenhead, says, " the Countesse, it seems, stole the Earls breeches, when he fled long since into the Isle of Man, and hath in his absence played the Man at Latham." This insinuation is certainly unjust; but the Earl seems to consider some explanation necessary, " why he left the land, when every gallant spirit had engaged himself for king and country." Danger of revolt and invasion of the island constitute the substance of this explanation. There is reason however to conjecture that he had been disappointed of the command he had a right to expect, when he brought a considerable levy to join the king at York: any explanation, in short, might be listened to, except a doubt of his loyalty and ardent military spirit, which were above all impeachment.

[3] Published in Peck's Desiderata Curiosa, in 1779.

[4] Peck, p. 446,—fortiter calumniari aliquid adhærebit.

[5] Peck, 446. " Loth to dwell too long on one subject," skip over to some other matter.

of determining the relative dates of his facts, which must accordingly be supplied by internal evidence, and in some cases by conjecture.

He appears to have been drawn thither, in 1643, by letters[6] intimating the danger of a revolt : the " people had begun the fashion of England in murmuring;" " assembled in a tumultuous manner; desiring new laws, they would have no bishops, pay no tithes to the clergie, despised authority, rescued people committed by the Governor," &c. &c.

The Earl's first care was to apply himself to the consideration of these insurrectionary movements; and as he found some interruption to his proceedings in the conduct of *Edward Christian*,[7] an attempt shall be made, so far as our limits will admit, to extract the Earl's own account of this person. " I was newly [8] got acquainted with

---

[6] Peck, p. 434.

[7] For a history of this family established in the Isle of Man so early as 1422, see Hutchinson's History of Cumberland, vol. iii. p. 146. They had previously been established in Wigtonshire.

[8] This is an example of the difficulty of arranging the relative dates: the word *newly*, thus employed at the earliest in 1643, refers to 1628, the date of the appointment of E. Christian to be governor of the Isle of Man, which office he held till 1635, (Sacheverill's account of the Isle of Man, published in 1702, p. 100.) The Earl being then Lord Strange, but apparently taking the lead in public business during his father's lifetime.

Captain Christian, whom I perceived to have abilities enough to do me service. I was told he had made a good fortune in the Indies, that he was a Mankesman borne." -- " He is excellent good companie; as rude as a sea captain should be; but refined as one that had civilized himself half a year at Court, where he served the Duke of Buckingham." -- " While he governed here some few years he pleased me very well," &c. &c. " But such is the condition of man, that most will have some fault or other to blurr all their best vertues; and his was of that condition which is reckoned with drunkenness, viz. *covetousness*, both marked *with age* to increase and grow in man." -- " When a Prince has given all, and the favourite can desire no more, they both grow weary of one another."[9]

---

[9] Peck, p. 444. There is apparently some error in Hutchinson's genealogy of the family in his History of Cumberland: 1st brother, John, born 1602; 2d died young; 3d William, born 1608; 4th Edward, Lieut. Governor of the Isle of Man, 1629, (according to Sacheverill, p. 160, 1628.) This Edward's birth cannot be placed earlier than 1609, and he could not well have made a fortune in the Indies, have frequented the court of Charles I., and be selected as a fit person to be a governor, at the age of 19 or 20. The person mentioned in the text was obviously of *mature age*; and *Edward the governor* appears to have been the younger brother of *William Christian*, a branch of the same family, possessing the estate of Knockrushen, near

An account of the Earl's successive public meetings, short, from the limits of our sketch, is extracted in a note [10] from the headings of the chapters (apparently composed by Peck.) In the last of these meetings it appears that Edward Christian attempted at its close to recapitulate

---

Castle Rushen, who, as well as Edward, was imprisoned in Peel Castle in 1643.

[10] Peck 338, et seq. Chap. viii. "The Earl appoints a meeting of the natives, every man to give in his grievances; upon which some think to outwit him, which he winks at, being not ready for them, therefore cajoles and divides them; on the appointed day he appears with a good guard; the people give in their complaints quietly and retire, Chap. ix. Another meeting appointed, when he also appears with a good guard. Many busy men speak only Mankes, which a more designing person (probably Captain Christian, a late governor) would hinder, but the Earl forbids it; advice about appearing in public; the Mankesmen great talkers and wranglers; the Earl's spies get in with them and wheedle them. Chap. x. The night before the meeting the Earl consults with his officers what to answer; but tells them nothing of his spies; compares both reports, and keeps back his own opinion; sends some of the officers, who he knew would be troublesome, out of the way, about other matters; the (present) governor afresh commended; what counsellors the properest. Chap. xi. The Earl's carriage to the people at his first going over; his carriage at the meeting to modest petitioners, to impudent, to the most confident, and to the most dangerous, viz. them who stood behind and prompted others. All things being agreed, Captain Christian cunningly begins disturbance; the Earl's reply and speech to the people; Christian is stroke blank; several people committed to prison and fined, which quiets them."

the business of the day: "Asked if we did not agree thus and thus," mentioning some things (says the Earl) " he had instructed the people to ask; which happily they had forgot." The Earl accordingly rose in wrath, and, after a short speech, "bade the court to rise, and no man to speak more."—"Some (he adds) were *committed to prison*, and there abided, until, upon *submission* and assurance of *being very good* and *quiet*, they were released, and others were put into their rooms.—I thought fit to make them be *deeply fined*; since this they all come in most submisse and *loving manner*."[11] Pretty efficient means of producing *quiet*, if the despot be strong enough, and with it such *love* as suits a despot's fancy! Among the prisoners were *Edward Christian* and his brother William of Knockrushen; the latter was released in 1644, on giving bond, among other conditions, *not to depart the island without licence.*

Of Edward, the Earl says, "I will return unto Captain Christian, whose business must be heard next week" (either in 1644 or early in 1645.) "*He is still in prison*, and I believe many wonder

---

[11] Peck, 442.

thereat, as savoring of injustice, and that his trial should be deferred so long." "Also his business is of that condition that *it concerns not himself alone.*" "If a Jurie of the people do passe upon him (being he had so cajoled them to believe he suffers for their sakes,) it is likely they should quit him, and then might he laugh at us, whom I had rather he had betrayed." "I remember one said it was much safer to take mens lives than their estates: for their children will sooner much forget the death of their father than the loss of their patrimonie."[12] Edward *died in custody* in Peel Castle in 1650,[13] after an imprisonment of between seven and eight years; and so far, at least, no ground can be discovered for that gratitude which is afterwards said to have been violated by this family, unless indeed we transplant ourselves to those countries where it is the fashion to flog a public officer one day and replace him in authority the next.

The insular records detail with minuteness the

---

[12] Peck, 448-9.
[13] Feltham's Tour, p. 161, places this event (while a prisoner in Peel Castle,) on the authority of a tombstone, in 1660, "John Greenhalgh being governor." Now John Greenhalgh ceased to be governor in 1651; the date is probably an error in the press for 1650.

complaints of the people relative to the exactions of the church, and their adjustment by a sort of public arbitration in October 1643. But it is singular, that neither in these records, nor in the Earl's very studied narrative, of the modes of discussion, the offences, and the punishments, is one word to be found regarding the more important points actually at issue between himself and the people. The fact, however, is fully developed, as if by accident, in one of the Chapters (xvi.) of this very desultory but sagacious performance. "There comes this very instant an occasion to me to acquaint you with a special matter, which, if by reason of these troublesome and dangerous times, I cannot bring to passe my intents therein, you may in your better leisure consider thereof, and make some use hereafter of my present labors, in the matter of a certain holding in this country, called the tenure of the straw;[14] where-

---

[14] In the transfer of real estates both parties came into the common law court, and the grantor in the face of the court transferred his title to the purchaser by the delivery of a straw; which being recorded, was his title. The same practice prevailed in the transfer of personal property. Sir Edward Coke, IV. 69, when speaking of the Isle of Man, says, " upon the sale of a horse, or any contract for any other thing, they make the stipulation perfect per *traditionem stipulæ*," (by the delivery of a straw.) Perhaps a more feasible etymology of *stipulation*, than

by *men thinke their dwellings are their own auntient inheritances*, and that they may passe the same to any, and dispose thereof *without license* from the Lord, but paying him a bare small rent like unto a fee-farme in England: wherein they are much deceived."

William the Conqueror, among his plans *for the benefit of his English subjects*, adopted that of inducing or compelling them to surrender their allodial lands, and receive them back to hold by feudal tenure. The Earl of Derby projected the surrender of a similar right, in order to create tenures more profitable to himself—a simple lease for three lives, or twenty-one years. The measure was entirely novel, although the attempt to prevent [15] alienation without license from the

---

the usual derivation from stipes (a stake or land mark,) or stips (a piece of money or wages.)

[15] Among those instances in which "the commands of the lord proprietor have (in the emphatic words of the commissioners of 1791, p. 67,) been *obtruded* on the people as laws," we find, in 1583, the prohibition to dispose of lands without license of the lord, is prefaced by the broad admission, that "contrary to good and laudable order, and diverse and sundry general restraints made, the inhabitants *have*, and *dayly do*, notwithstanding the said restrainte, *buy, sell, give, grant, chop* and *exchange* their farms, *lands, tenements*, &c. *at their liberties and pleasures.*" Alienation fines were first exacted in 1643. Report of Commissioners of 1791. App. A. No. 71, Rep. of Law Officers.

Lord, for purposes of a less profitable exaction, may be traced, together with the scenes of violence it produced through many passages in the ancient records, which would be inexplicable without this clue.

The Earl proceeded certainly with sufficient energy and considerable skill to the accomplishment of his object. In the very year of his arrival, Dec. 1643, he appointed commissioners[16] to compound for leases, consisting of some of his principal officers (members of council,) who had themselves been prevailed on by adequate considerations to surrender their estates, and are by general tradition accused of having conspired to delude their simple countrymen into the persuasion, that having no title-deeds, their estates were insecure; that leases were title-deeds; and although nominally for limited terms, declared the lands to be descendible to their eldest sons. It is remarkable that the names of *Ewan* and *William Christian*, two of the council, are alone excluded from this commission.

We have already seen two of the name committed to prison. The following notices, which

---

[16] The governor-comtroller, receiver; and John Cannel, deemster.

abundantly unfold the ground of the Earl's hostility to the name of Christian, relate to Ewan Christian, the father of William Dhône, and one of the Deemsters, excluded from the commission. "One presented me a petition against Deemster[17] Christian, on the behalf of an infant who is conceived to have a right unto his Farme Rainsway (Ronaldsway,) one of the principal holdings in this country, who, by reason of his eminencie here, and that he holdeth much of the same tenure of the straw in other places, he is soe observed, that certainly as I temper the matter with him in this, soe shall I prevail with others.[18] - - - - By policie[19] they (the Christians) are crept into the principal places of power, and they be seated round about the country, and in the heart of it; they are matched with the best families," &c.

"The prayer of the petition[20] formerly mentioned was to this effect, that there might be a fair tryal, and *when the right was recovered*, that

---

[17] Deemster, evidently Anglicized, the person who deems the law, a designation anciently unknown among the natives, who continue to call this officer *Brehon*, identical with the name of those judges and laws so often mentioned in the Histories of Ireland.

[18] Peck, 447.   [19] Ib. 448.

[20] I have ascertained the date of this petition to be 1643.

I would graunt them a lease thereof—this being in the tenure of the straw. - - - Upon some conference with the petitioner, I find a motion heretofore was made by my commissioners, that the Deemster should give this fellow a summe of money. But he would part with none, neverthelesse now it may be he will, and I hope be so wise as to assure unto himself his holding, by compounding with me for the lease of the same, to which, if they two agree, I shall grant it him on easy terms. For if he breake the ice, I may haply catch some fish."[21]

The issue of this piscatory project was but too successful. Ewan bent to the *reign of terror*, and gave up Ronaldsway to his son William, who accepted the lease, and named his own descendants for the lives. Still the objects attained were unsubstantial, as being contrary to all law, written or oral; and the system was incomplete,

---

[21] *Covetousness* is not attributed to this head of the family; but the Earl makes himself merry with his gallantry—natural children, it seems, took the name of their father, and not of their mother, as elsewhere, and " the deemster did not get soe many for lusts sake, as to make the name of Christian flourish." Of him, or a successor of the same name, it is related, that he " won 500*l*. at play from the Bishop of Sodor and Man, with which he purchased the manor of *Ewanrigg* in Cumberland, still possessed by that family."

until sanctioned by the semblance of legislative confirmation.

We have seen that the Earl had in the island a considerable military force, and we know from other sources [22] that they lived in a great measure at free quarters. We have his own testimony for stating, that he achieved his objects by imprisoning, until his prisoners "*promised to be good;*" and successively filling their places with others, until they also *conformed to his theory of public virtue.* And the reader will be prepared to hear without surprise, that the same means enabled him, in 1645, to arrange a legislature [23] capable of yielding a forced assent to this notable system of submission and loving kindness.

This is perhaps the most convenient place for stating, that in the subsequent surrender of the Island to the troops of the Parliament, the only stipulation made by the Islanders was, " that they might enjoy their lands and liberties as they formerly had." In what manner this stipulation was performed, my notes do not enable me to

---

[22] Evidence on the mock trial of William Dhône.

[23] We shall see, by and by, a very simple method of packing a judicial and legislative body, by removing and replacing *seven ndividuals* by one and the same mandate.

state. The restoration of Charles II., propitious in other respects, inflicted on the Isle of Man the revival of its feudal government; and the affair of the tenures continued to be a theme of perpetual contest and unavailing complaint, until finally adjusted in 1703, through the mediation of the excellent Bishop Wilson in a legislative compromise, known by the name of the Act of Settlement, whereby the people obtained a full recognition of their ancient rights, on condition of doubling the actual quit rents, and consenting to alienation fines, first exacted by the Earl James in 1643.[24]

In 1648, William Dhône was appointed Receiver General; and in the same year we find his elder brother, John (Assistant Deemster to his father Ewan,) committed to Peel Castle on one of these occasions, which strongly marks the character of the person and the times, and affords also a glimpse at the feeling of the people, and at the condition of the devoted family of Christian. The inquisitive will find it in a note;[25] other readers will pass on.

---

[24] Report of 1791, App. A. No. 71.
[25] A person named Charles Vaughan is brought to lodge an information, that being in England, he fell into company with a

The circumstances are familiarly known, to the reader of English history, of the march of the Earl of Derby in 1651, with a corps from the Isle of Man for the service of the King; his joining the royal army on the eve of the battle of Worcester; his flight and imprisonment at Chester, after that signal defeat; and his trial and execution at Bolton in Lancashire by the officers of the Parliament, on the 15th October of that year.

Immediately afterwards, Colonel Duckenfield, who commanded at Chester on behalf of the Parliament, proceeded with an armament of ten ships,

---

young man named Christian, who said he had lately left the Isle of Man, and was in search of a brother, who was clerk to a Parliament Officer; that in answer to some questions, he said, "The Earl did use the inhabitants of that Isle very hardly; had estreated great fines from the inhabitants; had changed the ancient tenures, and *forced* them to take leases. That he had taken away one hundred pounds a year from his father, and had kept his uncle in prison four or five years. But if ever the Earl came to England, (he had used the inhabitants so hardly,) that he was sure they would never suffer him to land in that Island again." An order is given to imprison John Christian (probably the reputed head of the family, his father being advanced in years,) in Peel Castle, until he entered into bonds to be of good behaviour, and *not to depart the Isle without license.*—(Insular Records.) The young man in question is said to have been the son of William Christian, of Knockrushen.

and a considerable military force, for the reduction of the Isle of Man.

William Christian was condemned and executed in 1662-3, for acts connected with its surrender, twelve years before, which are still involved in obscurity; and it will be most acceptable to the general reader that we should pass over the intermediate period,[26] and leave the facts regarding this individual, all of them extra-

---

[26] Some readers may desire an outline of this period. The lordship of the Island was given to Lord Fairfax, who deputed commissioners to regulate its affairs: one of them (Chaloner) published an account of the Island in 1656. He puts down William Christian as Receiver General in 1653. We find his name, as Governor, from 1656 to 1658, (Sacheverill. p. 101) in which year he was succeeded by Chaloner himself. Among the anomalies of those times, it would seem that he had retained the office of Receiver while officiating as Governor; and episcopacy having been abolished, and the receipts of the see added to those of the exchequer, he had large accounts to settle, for which Chaloner sequestered his estates in his absence, and imprisoned and held to bail his brother John, for aiding what he calls his escape: his son George returned from England, by permission of Lord Fairfax, to settle his father's accounts. Chaloner informs us, that the revenues of the suppressed see were *not appropriated* to the private use of Lord Fairfax, who, " for the better encouragement and support of the Ministers of the Gospel and for the promoting of learning, hath conferred all this revenue upon the Ministers, and also for maintaining free schools, *i. e.* at Castletown, Peel, Douglass, and Ramsay." Chaloner pays a liberal tribute to the talents of the clergy, and the learning and piety of the late bishops.]

ordinary, and some of peculiar interest, to be developed by the record of the trial, and documents derived from other sources.

A mandate by Charles, 8th Earl of Derby, dated at Latham in September 1662, after descanting on the heinous sin of rebellion, " aggravated by its being instrumental[27] in the death of the Lord," and stating that he is himself concerned to revenge a father's blood," orders William Christian to be proceeded against forthwith, for all his illegal actions at, before, or after, the year 1651, (a pretty sweeping range.) The indictment charges him with " being the head of an insurrection against the countess of Derby in 1651, assuming the power unto himself, and depriving her Ladyship, his Lordship, and heirs thereof."

A series of depositions appear on record from the 3d to the 13th October, and a reference by the precious depositaries of justice of that day, to the twenty-four Keys.[28] " Whether upon the

---

[27] See the remark in Christian's dying speech, that the late Earl had been executed eight days before the insurrection.

[28] The court for criminal trials was composed of the governor and council (including the deemsters) and the keys, who also, with the Lord, composed the three branches of the legisla-

examination taken and read before, you find Mr. W. Christian, of Ronaldsway, within compass of the statute of the year 1422, that is to receive a sentence *without quest*, or to be tried in the ordinary course of law." This body, designated on the record "so many of the Keys as were then present," were in number seventeen; but not being yet sufficiently select to approve of *sentence without trial*, made their return, To be tried by course of law.

On the 26th November, it is recorded, that the Governor and Attorney General having proceeded to the gaol " with a guard of soldiers, to require him (Christian) to the bar to receive his trial, he refused, and denied to come, and abide the same —(admirable courtesy to invite, instead of bringing him to the bar!) Whereupon the Governor demanded the law of Deemster Norris, who then sat in judication. Deemster John Christian having not appeared, and Mr. Edward Christian,[29]

---

tive body; and it was the practice in cases of doubt to refer points of customary law to the deemsters and keys.

[29] The grandson of *Evan*. It appears by the proceedings of the King in council, 1663, that " *he did, when the court refused to admit of the deceased William Christian's plea* of the Act of indemnity, *make his protestation* against their *illegal proceedings*, and did withdraw himself, and came to England to solicit his Majesty, and implore his justice."

his son, and assistant, having also *forborne to sit* in this Court, he the said Deemster Norris craved the advice and assistance of the twenty-four Keys; and the said Deemster and Keys deemed the law therein, to wit, that he is at the mercy of the Lord for life and goods.

It will be observed, that seven of the Keys were formerly absent, on what account we shall presently see. All this was very cleverly arranged by the following recorded order, 29th December— "*These of the twenty-four Keys are removed of that Company, in reference to my Honourable Lord's order in that behalf;*" enumerating seven names, not of the seventeen before mentioned, and naming seven others who " are sworn [30] in their places." The judicature is farther improved by transferring an eighth individual of the first seventeen to the council, and filling his place with another proper person. These facts have been related with some minuteness of detail for two reasons: 1st, Although nearly equalled by some of the subsequent proceedings, they would

---

[30] The Commissioners of 1791 are in doubt regarding the time when, and the manner in which, the keys were first elected: this notable precedent had perhaps not fallen under their observation.

not be credited on common authority; and 2d, They render all comment unnecessary, and prepare the reader for any judgment, however extraordinary, to be expected from such a tribunal.

Then come the proceedings of the 29th December—The Proposals, as they are named, to the Deemsters,[31] and twenty-four Keys now assembled, " to be answered in point of law." " 1st, Any malefactor, &c. being indicted, &c. and denying to abide the law of his country in that course, (notwithstanding any argument or plea he may offer for himself,) and thereupon deemed to forfeit body and goods, &c. whether he may afterwards obtain the same benefit, &c. &c.;" to which, on the same day, they answered in the negative. It was found practicable, on the 31st, to *bring* the prisoner to the bar, to hear his sentence of being " *shot to death, that thereupon his life may depart from his body,*" which sentence was executed on the 2d of January 1663.

That he made " an excellent speech" at the place of execution, is recorded, where we should little expect to find it, in the Parochial Register;

---

[31] Hugh Cannel was now added as a second deemster.

the accuracy of that which has been preserved as such in the family of a clergyman, (and appears to have been printed on or before 1776,[32]) rests chiefly on internal evidence; and on its accordance, in some material points, with facts suppressed or distorted in the Records, but established in the proceedings of the Privy Council. It is therefore given without abbreviation, and the material points of evidence in the voluminous depositions on both trials [33] are extracted for reference in a note.[34]

---

[32] One of the copies in my possession is stated to be transcribed in that year from the printed speech, the other as stated in the text.

[33] Both trials: the first is for the same purposes as the English grand jury, with this most especial difference, that evidence is admitted *for the prisoner*, and it thus becomes what it is frequently called, the first trial; the second, if the indictment be found, is in all respects like that by petty jury in England.

[34] This testimony will of course be received with due suspicion, and confronted with the only defence known, that of his dying speech. It goes to establish that Christian had placed himself at the head of an association bound by a secret oath, to " withstand the Lady of Derby in her designs until she had yielded or condescended to their aggrievances;" among which grievances, during the Earl's residence, we find, incidentally noticed, " the troop that was in the Isle and their free quarterage;" that he had represented her ladyship to have deceived him, by entering into negotiations with the parliament, contrary to her promise to communicate with him in such a case;

The last speech of William Christian, Esq. who was executed 2d January, 1662-3:

"Gentlemen, and the rest of you who have accompanied me this day to the gate of death,

---

that Christian and his associates declared that she was about to sell them for twopence or threepence a piece; that he told his associates, that he had entered into correspondence with Major Fox and the parliament, and received their authority to raise the country; that in consequence of this insurrection her ladyship appointed commissioners to treat with others " *on the part of the country,*" and articles of agreement were concluded (see the speech) which no where now appear; that on the appearance of Duckenfield's ships, standing for Ramsay Bay, one of the insurgents boarded them off Douglas, " to give intelligence of the condition of the country;" that the disposable troops marched under the governor, Sir Philip Musgrave, for Ramsay; that when the shipping had anchored, a deputation of three persons, *viz.* John Christian, Ewan Curphey, and William Standish, proceeded on board, to negotiate for the surrender of the Island (where William was does not appear.) The destruction of the articles of agreement, and the silence of the records regarding the relative strength of the forces, leave us without the means of determining the degree of merit or demerit to be ascribed to these negociators, or the precise authority under which they acted; but the grievances to be redressed, are cleared from every obscurity by the all-sufficient testimony of the terms demanded from the victors, "*that they might enjoy their lands and liberties as formerly they had;* and that it was demanded whether they asked any more, but nothing else was demanded that this examinant heard of." The taking of Loyal Fort near Ramsay, (commanded by a Major Duckenfield, who was made prisoner,) and of Peel Castle, appear on record; but nothing could be found regarding the *surrender of Castle Rushen, or of the Countess*

I know you expect I should say something at my departure; and indeed I am in some measure willing to satisfy you, having not had the least liberty, since my imprisonment, to acquaint any with the sadness of my sufferings, which flesh and blood could not have endured, without the power and assistance of my most gracious and good God, into whose hands I do now commit my poor soul, not doubting but that I shall very quickly be in the arms of his mercy.

---

of Derby's subsequent imprisonment. Had the often repeated tale, of William Christian having " treacherously seized upon the lady and her children, with the governors of both castles, in the middle of the night"—(Rolt's History of the Isle of Man, published in 1773, p. 89)—rested on the slightest semblance of truth, we should inevitably have found an attempt to prove it in the proceedings of this mock trial. In the absence of authentic details, the tradition may be adverted to, that her ladyship, on learning the proceedings at Ramsay, hastened to embark in a vessel she had prepared, but was intercepted before she could reach it. The same uncertainty exists with regard to any negotiations on her part, with the officers of the parliament, as affirmed by the insurgents; the Earl's first letter, after his capture and before his trial, says, "Truly, as matters go, it will be best for you to make conditions for yourself, children, and friends, in the manner as we have proposed, or as you can farther agree with Col. Duckenfield; who being so much a gentleman born, will doubtless, for his own honor, deal fairly with you." He seems also to have hoped at that time that it might influence his own fate: and the eloquent and affecting letter written immediately before his execution, repeats the same admonitions *to treat.*—Rolt. p. 74 and 84.

"I am, as you now see, hurried hither by the power of *a pretended court of justice*, the members whereof, or at least the greatest part of them, are by no means qualified, but very ill befitting their new places. The reasons you may give yourselves.

"The cause for which I am brought hither, as the *prompted* and *threatened* jury has delivered, is high treason against the Countess Dowager of Derby, for that I did, as they say, in the year fifty-one, raise a force against her for the suppressing and rooting out that family. How unjust the accusation is, very few of you that hear me this day but can witness; and *that the then rising of the people*, in which afterwards I came to be engaged, did not at all, or in the least degree, intend the prejudice or ruin of that family; *the chief whereof being, as you well remember, dead eight days, or thereabout, before that action happened*. But the true cause of that rising, as [35] *the jury did twice bring in*, was to present grievances to our Honourable Lady; which was done by me, and afterwards approved by her

---

[35] This fact, as might be expected, is not to be traced on the record of the trial.

Ladyship, under the hand of her then Secretary, M. Trevach, who is yet living, *which agreement hath since, to my own ruin and my poor family's endless sorrow, been forced from me.* The Lord God forgive them the injustice of their dealings with me, and I wish from my heart it may not be laid to their charge another day.

"You now see me here *a sacrifice ready to be offered up for that which was the preservation of your lives and fortunes, which were then in hazard, but that I stood between you and your* (then in all appearance) *utter ruin.* I wish you still may, as hitherto, enjoy the sweet benefit and blessing of peace, though from that minute until now I have still been prosecuted and persecuted, nor have I ever since found a place to rest myself in. But my God be for ever blessed and praised, who hath given me so large a measure of patience!

"What services I have done for that Noble Family, by whose power I am now to take my latest breath, I dare appeal to themselves, whether I have not deserved better things from some of them, than the sentence of my bodily destruction, and seizure of the poor estate my son ought to enjoy, being purchased and left him by his grandfather. It might have been much better had I not spent it in the service of my Honourable Lord of Derby and his family; these things I need not mention to you, for that most of you are witnesses to it. I shall now beg your patience while I tell you here, in the presence of God, that I never in all my life acted any thing with intention to prejudice my Sovereign Lord the King, nor the late Earl of Derby, nor the now Earl; yet notwithstanding, *being in England at the time* of his sacred Majesty's happy restoration, I went to London, with many others, to have a sight of my gracious King, whom God preserve, and whom until then I never had seen. But I was not long there when I was arrested upon an action of twenty thousand pounds, and clapped up in the Fleet; unto which action, I being a stranger, could give no bail, but was there kept nearly a whole year. How I suffered God he knows; but at last, having gained my liberty, I thought good to advise with several gentlemen concerning his Majesty's gracious Act of Indemnity, that was then set forth, in which I thought myself concerned; unto which they told me, there was no doubt to be made but that all actions committed in the Isle of Man, relating in any kind to the war, were pardoned by the Act of Indemnity, and all other places within his Majesty's dominions and countries. Whereupon, and having been forced to absent myself from my poor wife and children near three years, being all that time under persecution, I did with great content and satisfaction return into this Island, hoping then to receive the comfort and sweet enjoyment of my friends and poor family. But alas! I have fallen into the snare of the fowler; but my God shall ever be praised,—though he kill me, yet will I trust in him.

"I may justly say no man in this Island knows better than myself the power the Lord Derby hath in this Island, subordinate to his sacred Majesty, of which *I have given a full account in my declaration presented to my judges, which I much fear will never see light,*[36] *which is no small trouble to me.*

"It was his Majesty's most gracious Act of Indemnity gave me the confidence and assurance of my safety; on which, and an appeal I made to his sacred Majesty and Privy Council, from the unjustness of the proceedings had against me, I

---

[36] The apprehension was but too correct.

did much rely, being his Majesty's subject here, and a denizen of England both by birth and fortune. And *in regard I have disobeyed the power of my Lord of Derby's Act of Indemnity, which you now look upon, and his Majesty's Act cast out as being of no force*, I have with greater violence been persecuted; yet nevertheless I do declare, that no subject whatever can or ought to take upon them acts of indemnity but his sacred Majesty only, with the confirmation of Parliament.

" It is very fit I should say something as to my education and religion. I think I need not inform you, for you all know, I was brought up a son of the Church of England, which was at that time in her splendour and glory; and to my endless comfort I have ever since continued a faithful member,—witness several of my actions in the late times of liberty. And as for government, I never was against monarchy, which now, to my soul's great satisfaction, I have lived to see is settled and established. I am well assured that men of upright life and conversation may have the favourable countenance of our gracious King, under whose happy government, God of his infinate mercy long continue these his kingdoms and

D

dominions. And now I do most heartily thank my good God that I have had so much liberty and time to disburden myself of several things that have laid heavy upon me all the time of my imprisonment, in which I have not had *time, or liberty, to speak or write* any of my thoughts; and from my soul I wish all animosity may after my death be quite laid aside, and my death by none be called in question, for I do freely forgive all that have had any hand in my persecution; and may our good God preserve you all in peace and quiet the remainder of your days.

" Be ye all of you his Majesty's liege people, loyal, and faithful to his sacred Majesty; and according to your oath of faith and fealty to my Honourable Lord of Derby, *do you likewise, in all just and lawful ways, observe* his commands; and know, that you must one day give an account of all your deeds. And now the blessing of Almighty God be with you all, and preserve you from violent death, and keep you in peace of conscience all your days.

" I will now hasten, for my flesh is willing to be dissolved, and my spirit to be with God, who hath given me full assurance of his mercy and pardon for all my sins, of which his unspeakable goodness and loving-kindness my poor soul is exceedingly satisfied."

Note.[37] Here he fell upon his knees, and passed some time in prayer; then rising exceedingly cheerful, he addressed the soldiers appointed for his execution, saying—" Now for you, who are appointed by lot my executioners, I do freely forgive you." He requested them and all present to pray for him; adding, " There is but a thin veil betwixt me and death; once more I request your prayers, for now I take my last farewell."

The soldiers wished to bind him to the spot on which he stood. He said, " Trouble not yourselves or me; for I that dare face death in whatever form he comes, will not start at your fire and bullets; nor can the power you have deprive me of my courage." At his desire a piece of white paper was given him, which with the utmost composure he pinned to his breast, to direct them where to aim; and after a short prayer addressed the soldiers thus—" Hit this, and you do your own and my work." And presently after, stretching forth his arms, which was the signal he gave them, he was shot through the heart and fell.

---

[37] This note is annexed to all the copies of the speech.

Edward Christian, the nephew, and George, the son of the deceased, lost no time in appealing to his Majesty in Council against this judicial murder; and George was furnished with an order " to pass and repass," &c. " and bring with him such records and persons as he should desire, to make out the truth of his complaint." Edward returned with him to the Island for that purpose; for we find him, in April 1663, compelled, in the true spirit of the day, to give bond " that he would at all times appear and answer to such charges as might be preferred against him, and *not depart the Isle without licence.*" George was prevented, by various contrivances, from serving the King's order; but on presenting a second petition, the Governor, Deemster, and Members of Council, were brought up to London by a Serjeant at Arms; and these six persons, together with the Earl of Derby, being compelled to appear, a full hearing took place before the King in person, the Chancellor, the Lord Chief Justice, Lord Chief Baron, and other Members of Council; judgment was extended on the 5th August, and that judgment was on the 14th of the same month ordered " to be printed in folio, in such manner as Acts of Parliament are usually printed, and his Majesty's Arms prefixed."

This *authentic document* designates the persons brought up as "*Members of the pretended Court of Justice;*" declares " that the general Act of Pardon and Amnesty did extend to the Isle of Man, and ought to have been taken notice of by the Judges in that Island, *although it had not been pleaded;* that the Court *refused to admit* the deceased William Christian's *plea* of the Act of Indemnity," &c. " Full restitution is ordered to be made to his heirs of all his estates, real and personal." Three[38] other persons " who were by the same Court of Justice imprisoned, and their estates *seized and confiscated without any legal trial,*" are ordered, together with the Christians, " to be restored to all their estates, real and personal, and to be fully repaired in all the charges and expenses which they have been at since their first imprisonment, as well in the prosecution of this business as in their journey hither, or in any other way thereunto relating." The mode of raising funds for the purposes of this

---

[38] Ewan Curphey, Samuel Ratcliffe, and John Cæsar, men of considerable landed property.

restitution is equally peculiar and instructive: these " sums of money are ordered to be furnished by the Deemsters, Members, and Assistants of the said Court of Justice," who are directed " to raise and make due payment thereof to the parties."

" And to the end that the blood that has been unjustly spilt may in some sort be expiated," &c. the Deemsters are ordered to be committed to the King's Bench to be proceeded against, &c. &c. and receive condign punishment. [It is believed that this part of the order was afterwards relaxed or rendered nugatory.] The three Members of Council were released on giving security to appear, if required, and to make the restitution ordered. " And in regard that Edward Christian, being one of the Deemsters or Judges in the Isle of Man, *did, when the Court refused to admit of the deceased W. Christian's plea of the Act of Indemnity, make his protestation against their illegal proceedings, and did withdraw himself, and come to England to solicit his Majesty and implore his justice,* It is ordered that the Earl of Derby do forthwith, by commission, &c. restore and appoint him as Deemster, so to remain and continue, &c. (which order was disobeyed.) And lastly, that Henry Nowell, Deputy Governor, whose fault hath been *the not complying with, and yielding due obedience to, the order[39] of his Majesty and this Board sent unto the Island*"—(O most lame and impotent conclusion!) " be permitted to return to the Isle, and enforce the present Order of the King in Council."

Of the Earl of Derby no farther mention occurs in this document. The sacrifices made by this noble family in support of the royal cause, drew a large share of indulgence over the exceptionable parts of their conduct; but the mortification necessarily consequent on this appeal, the incessant complaints of the people, and the difficulty subsequently experienced by them in obtaining access to a superior tribunal, receive a curious illustration in an order of the king in council, dated 20th August 1670, on a petition of the Earl of Derby, " that the clerk of the council in waiting receive no petition, appeal or complaint, *against the lord or government of the Isle of Man*, without having first good security from

---

[39] Tradition, in accordance with the dirge of William Dhône, says that the order to stop proceedings and suspend the sentence arrived on the day preceding that of his execution.

the complainant to answer costs, damages and charges."

The historical notices of this kingdom [40] of Lilliput are curious and instructive with reference to other times and different circumstances, and they have seemed to require little comment or antiquarian remark; but to condense what may be collected with regard to Edward Christian, the accomplished villain of Peveril; the insinuations of his accuser [41] constitute in themselves an abundant defence. When so little can be imputed by such an adversary, the character must indeed be invulnerable. Tradition ascribes to him nothing but what is amiable, patriotic, honourable and good, in all the relations of public and private life. He died, after an imprisonment of seven or eight years, the victim of incorrigible obstinacy according to one, of ruthless tyranny, according to another vocabulary; but resembling the character of the Novel in nothing but unconquerable courage.

Treachery and ingratitude have been heaped

---

[40] Earl James, although studious of kingcraft, assigns good reasons for having never pretended to assume that title, and among others, "Nor doth it please a king that any of his subjects should too much love that name, were it but to act in a play."—Peck, 436.   [41] Peck, passim.

on the memory of William Christian with sufficient profusion. Regarding the first of these crimes: if all that has been affirmed or insinuated in the mock trial, rested on a less questionable basis, posterity would scarcely pronounce an unanimous verdict, of moral and political guilt, against an association to subvert such a government as is described by its own author. The *peculiar* favours for which he or his family were ungrateful, are not to be discovered in these proceedings; except, indeed, in the form of " chastisements of the Almighty—blessings in disguise." But if credit be given to the dying words of William Christian, his efforts were strictly limited to a redress of grievances,—a purpose always criminal in the eye of the oppressor. If he had lived and died on a larger scene, his memory would probably have survived among the patriots and the heroes. In some of the manuscript narratives he is designated as a *martyr* for the rights and liberties of his countrymen; who add, in their homely manner, that he was condemned without trial, and murdered without remorse.

We have purposely abstained from all attempt to enlist the passions in favour of the sufferings of a people, or in detestation of oppressions, which ought, perhaps, to be ascribed as much to the character of the times as to that of individuals. The naked facts of the case (unaided by the wild and plaintive notes in which the maidens of the isle were wont to bewail "*the* [42] *heart rending death of fair-haired William,*") are sufficient of themselves to awaken the sympathy of every generous mind; and it were a more worthy exercise of that despotic power over the imagination, so eminently possessed by the Great Unknown, to embalm the remembrance of two such men in his immortal pages, than to load their memories with crimes, such as no human being ever committed.

---

[42] The literal translation given to me by a young lady.

Printed by Libri Plureos GmbH in Hamburg, Germany